ON THE HAPPY LIFE

ON THE HAPPY LIFE

ST. AUGUSTINE OF HIPPO

Copyright 2021 by Dalcassian Press

All rights reserved. No part of this book may be reproduced in any manner whatsoever without written permission except in the case of brief quotations embodied in critical articles and reviews.

No part of this publication may be reproduced, distributed, or transmitted in any form or by any means, including photocopying, recording, or other electronic or mechanical methods, without the prior written permission of the publisher, except in the case of brief quotations embodied in critical reviews and certain other non-commercial uses permitted by copyright law. For permission request, write to Dalcassian Press at admin@thescriptoriumproject.com

Translator: Curtin, D.P. (1985-)

ISBN: 979-8-3302-3384-7 (Paperback)
ISBN: 979-8-3302-3014-3 (eBook)
Library of Congress Control Number:

Printed by Ingram Content Group, 1 Ingram Blvd, La Vergne, Tennessee
First Printing 2021, Dalcassian Press, Wilmington, DE

This work is part of a series produced in association with the Scriptorium Project and its community of scholars and translators.
Please visit our website at: www.thescriptoriumproject.com

INTRODUCTION

St. Augustine's *De Beata Vita* (*On the Happy Life*) is one of the earliest philosophical dialogues of the Church Father, written shortly after his conversion to Christianity in 386 AD. Set within the intimate and discursive context of a family celebration—his mother Monica's birthday—the work reveals Augustine's developing theological convictions, his Platonic inheritance, and his enduring concern with the nature of true happiness. Though brief, the dialogue poses complex moral and theological questions that resonate deeply in today's world: What is happiness? Can it be found in this life? Is it self-sufficient, or does it require divine grace? St. Augustine's treatment of these themes offers profound insights, particularly as modern society continues to search for meaning in a fractured, materialistic world.

At the heart of *De Beata Vita* is St. Augustine's exploration of the question: *What is happiness?* The dialogue's participants—his friends and family—initially propose conventional answers: happiness consists in possessing what one desires, or in having material goods, or perhaps in the pursuit of knowledge. But Augustine gently leads the discussion toward a more profound conclusion: true happiness is not in *having*, but in *being*—specifically, in being rightly ordered toward God. He writes: "Happy is he who possesses God." This radical proposition confronts not only ancient philosophies that equated happiness with virtue (e.g., the Stoics), but also modern consumerist assumptions that link happiness with wealth, pleasure, or success. St. Augustine argues that anything transient, anything that can be lost, cannot constitute true beatitude. Happiness must be eternal, immutable, and secure.

This notion presents a powerful moral challenge to the modern age. In a culture addicted to dopamine, distraction, and digital gratification, St. Augustine's insistence that only the eternal and unchangeable can bring true satisfaction is a bracing critique. His view invites a reorientation of desire: not away from joy, but toward its only proper and lasting object—God.

A central tension in *De Beata Vita* is the role of human reason versus divine revelation. While St. Augustine engages in rational argumentation in the Platonic style, he increasingly leans toward a theology that recognizes the limitations of reason unaided by faith. This tension reflects Augustine's own intellectual journey—from the rationalism of Neoplatonism to the humility of Christian belief. He acknowledges that the intellect has a role in guiding the soul toward truth, but also that human knowledge is darkened by sin. Hence, he introduces a moral dimension to epistemology: it is not only intelligence that finds truth, but the pure of heart. As he writes, "He who loves God is happy." The beatific life is not merely a mental state but a moral condition. This raises a crucial theological question: Is happiness accessible to all, or only to the morally upright? And is it a matter of achievement or of grace?

Augustine's answer evolves toward the latter. While he retains the Platonic framework of ascent toward the good, he increasingly emphasizes the necessity of grace. The happy life, then, is not the fruit of unaided effort, but of divine illumination and love. In this sense, St. Augustine anticipates major themes of his later works, especially *Confessions* and *The City of God*. In the modern world, where reason is often exalted as the ultimate authority, St. Augustine's acknowledgment of its limits—and his invitation to humility before the divine—remains highly relevant. The rise of mental health crises, existential anxiety, and spiritual malaise suggests that rationality alone does not satisfy the soul's deepest longings.

Throughout the dialogue, St. Augustine subtly contrasts temporal goods with eternal goods. He critiques the desire for riches, pleasure, and even intellectual pride. In their place, he posits the good that never fails: communion with God. This raises a persistent moral question: What are we living for? The characters in the dialogue debate whether wealth or leisure can make one happy, but Augustine insists that such goods are only means, and that the end must be higher. In this, Augustine anticipates later Christian moral teaching about detachment, simplicity, and the alignment of one's will with divine will. This is not to say St. Augustine rejects the world entirely. Rather, he warns against disordered love—*amor sui* (love of self) over *amor Dei* (love of God). The real moral dilemma, then, is not between material and spiritual, but between the properly ordered and disordered soul. In contemporary life, where identity is often built around career, possessions, or digital persona, Augustine's ethical vision is a countercultural call to simplicity, humility, and devotion. It is also an implicit critique of the loneliness and exhaustion that comes from constantly chasing external validation.

The dialogical form of *De Beata Vita* is itself a moral and theological statement. St. Augustine chooses to explore truth not through solitary meditation, but through conversation with friends and family. This models the Christian understanding of knowledge as relational, not individualistic. It also underscores the importance of community in the moral life. Notably, St. Augustine's mother Monica plays a central role—not as a silent woman in the background, but as a voice of wisdom and joy. Her inclusion in the dialogue is not merely personal but symbolic: the beatific life is accessible not only to philosophers but to all who seek God with sincerity. This is an important theological corrective in a world that often sees religion as esoteric or exclusionary. For St. Augustine, happiness is not the privilege of the elite but the vocation of every human being. Moreover, the setting—a meal shared among loved ones—suggests a sacramental vision of life. Even in early writings, Augustine hints at the Eucharistic reality that undergirds Christian joy: that Christ gives himself to us not only spiritually but physically, in the context of community and love.

Augustine's *De Beata Vita* may be over 1,600 years old, but it's themes remain urgently relevant. In an age marked by anxiety, alienation, and an ever-expanding market of pseudo-happiness, St. Augustine's vision of beatitude grounded in eternal truth offers a radical alternative. His insights challenge various modern assumptions-

firstly, that happiness is subjective—St. Augustine insists it is objective, and by extension found only in God.; secondly, that more is better—St. Augustine urges a sense of studied detachment and simplicity in our lives; finally that knowledge alone is enough—St. Augustine points to love and grace as the key.

In our time, when truth is often relativized and happiness commercialized, *De Beata Vita* invites us back to the fundamentals: What are we made for? Who are we becoming? What—or whom—do we love most? In the end, Augustine's conclusion is disarmingly simple: "To live happily is nothing other than to possess eternal life, to know God, to be like God." This is not just a philosophical claim but a moral imperative and a theological hope. It is a call to reorient our lives toward the source of all joy—a call that still echoes across the centuries.

1

CHAPTER ONE

Preface. *He addresses the book to Theodore, revealing to him the winds that have driven him to the harbor of Christian philosophy. The occasion for the discussion.*

1. If to the harbor of philosophy, from which we now proceed solely into the realm of the blessed life, a most humane and great man, Theodore, were to be led by a well-structured course of reason and by his very will; I do not know whether I may rashly say that far fewer men would have reached it, although even now, as we see, very few indeed arrive there. For when into this world, whether by God, or by nature, or by necessity, or by our own will, or by some combination of these, or by all of them together (for the matter is very obscure, but nonetheless it has been taken up by you to be illuminated), as if cast into a certain stormy sea, how few would know where they ought to strive, or whither they should return, unless sometimes a tempest, which seems adverse to the foolish, would force them, against their will and struggling, into the most desirable land, while they wander unknowingly?

2. Therefore, among the men whom philosophy can receive, I seem to see three kinds of sailors. One is of those who, when the age has as-

sumed the faculty of reason, flee with little impulse and push of the oars from nearby, and hide themselves in that tranquility, from where they raise the clearest sign of some work to the other citizens whom they can admonish. The second, however, is the opposite of the first, who, deceived by the most deceptive appearance of the sea, choose to advance into the midst and dare to wander far from their homeland, often forgetting it. If by some hidden means, from the stern, a wind, which they think favorable, has pursued them, they penetrate into the depths of miseries, elated and rejoicing that the most deceptive serenity of pleasures and honors flatters them from every side. What else can be desired for these, except that they may be caught by certain adverse things from which they have been thrown, and if that is not enough, may a raging tempest and contrary wind lead them to certain and solid joys, or to weeping and lamenting? However, many of this kind have not yet wandered far, and some are brought back by not so serious troubles. These are the men who, when either the lamentable tragedies of their fortunes or the anxious difficulties of vain affairs, having nothing else to do, have thrust them into the books of the most learned and wise men, awaken in a certain manner in that harbor, from where no promises of that laughing sea, which is too false, may exclude them. There is, however, a third kind among these, those who either at the very threshold of youth or having long been tossed about, still look back at certain signs, and remember their sweetest homeland, even amidst the waves: and either by a straight course, without any falsehood, and without delay, they return to it; or often, either wandering among the clouds, or contemplating sinking stars, or being captivated by certain temptations, delaying the times of good navigation, they wander longer, often even in peril. These, too, are often compelled by some calamity in their fluctuating fortunes, as if an adverse tempest to their efforts, to return to their most desired and peaceful homeland.

3. However, before all those who are drawn in any way to the region of blessed life, there stands an immense mountain directly before the port itself, which also creates great difficulties for those approaching, and is to be feared most vehemently and avoided most cautiously. For it shines so brightly, and is clothed in that deceptive light, that it not only presents itself as a place to inhabit for those arriving and not yet entering, promising to satisfy their wishes for the very blessed land; but often invites men from the port itself to itself, and sometimes detains those delighted by its great height, from which they may wish to look down upon others. Yet these often warn those coming not to be deceived by hidden rocks beneath, nor to think it easy to ascend to it; and they kindly teach how they may enter without danger due to the proximity of that land. Thus, while they envy them the vainest glory, they show them a place of safety. For what other mountain does reason wish to be understood as to be feared by those approaching philosophy, except the proud pursuit of empty glory, which has so little that is full and solid within, that it sinks and absorbs those inflated by it, walking upon fragile ground, and, when they are rolled into darkness, snatches away the most resplendent home, which they had almost already seen?

4. Since these things are so, receive this, my Theodore, for in what I desire, I see you alone, and I always admire you as most suitable; receive, I say, both what kind of those three types of men has given me to you, and in what place I seem to be, and what kind of help I confidently expect from you. From my nineteenth year of age, after I received that book of Cicero, which is called Hortensius, in the school of rhetoric, I was so inflamed with love for philosophy that I immediately contemplated transferring myself to it. But neither did I lack the mists that confused my course; and for a long time, I confess, I was led into error, gazing at the stars sliding into the ocean. For a certain childish superstition frightened me from the very inquiry: and when I became more upright, I dispelled that darkness, and persuaded

myself to believe in those teaching rather than commanding; I fell in with men for whom this light which is seen by the eyes seemed to be among the highest and divine things to be revered. I did not agree, but I thought they were concealing something great in those wrappings, which they would one day reveal. But when I escaped from them, especially after crossing that sea, for a long time my rudder held me, resisting all winds in the midst of the waves of the Academy. Then I came to these lands; here I learned whom I should trust. For I observed both often in our priest and sometimes in your speeches, when God was being considered, that nothing of the body should be thought at all, nor when the soul was considered: for that is the one thing closest to God among things. But lest I quickly fly into the lap of philosophy, I confess I was detained by the allure of honor from my wife; so that having attained these things, at last I might, which has been allowed to very few most fortunate, sail with all sails and oars into that bay, and there find rest. After reading a very few books of Plato, of whom I have heard you are most eager, and comparing them, as much as I could, also with the authority of those who have handed down divine mysteries, I became so inflamed that I wished to break all those anchors, unless the opinion of certain men moved me (Conf. lib. 7, capp. 9, 20). What then remained except that the storm, which was thought to be adverse, should come to my aid while I lingered over the superfluous? And thus such pain seized my heart that, unable to bear the burden of that profession, by which I perhaps was sailing to the Sirens, I cast away everything, and would bring the desired tranquility even to a ship shaken and torn.

5. Therefore, you see in what philosophy I sail as if in a port. But it also lies open wide, and its magnitude, although now less dangerous, does not entirely exclude error. For to which part of the land, which is indeed the one blessed, should I approach and touch, I do not know at all. For what solid thing do I hold, while the question of the soul still wavers and fluctuates? Therefore, I beseech you by your virtue, by

your humanity, by the bond and commerce of souls among themselves, to extend your right hand. This, however, is that you love me, and believe that you are loved in return by me and held dear. If I obtain this, I will very easily approach the very blessed life, which I presume you already cling to, with little effort. But what should I do, or how should I gather my necessities to that port so that you may know, and from it my mind (for I find no other signs by which I may show myself) so that you may more fully understand, the beginning of my discussions, which seems to me to have escaped more religiously, and to be worthier of your title, I thought it fitting to write to you, and to dedicate it by your very name. Indeed very aptly; for we have inquired among ourselves about the blessed life, and I see nothing else that should be called a gift of God more. I am not terrified by your eloquence; for whatever I love, although I do not attain it, I cannot fear: much less the height of fortune; for with you indeed, although it is great, it is favorable; for those whom it rules, it makes those very same ones favorable. But now what should I bring, I ask you, pay attention.

6. On the Idus of November, it was my birthday: after such a light lunch, that nothing of the mind was hindered by it, I called together all those who not only on that day but daily dined with me, to sit in the baths; for a place suitable to the time and secluded had occurred. Among them, I do not hesitate to name them for your singular kindness, first of all my mother, whose merit I believe to be the reason for all that I am while I live; my brother Navigius, Trygetius and Licentius, my fellow citizens and students; nor did I wish to leave out my cousins Lastidianus and Rustic, although they have suffered nothing even of grammar, for I considered their common sense necessary for the matter I was preparing. There was also with us the youngest of all in age, but whose talent, if I am not mistaken in my affection, promises something great, my son Adeodatus. With these matters in mind, I began thus.

2

CHAPTER TWO

First day's discussion. *We are composed of soul and body. Food is necessary for the body. The soul also has its food. A person is not happy who does not have what they want. Yet not everyone who has what they want is happy. What should a person compare to be happy? Who has God. An academic cannot be happy, therefore neither can a wise person.*

7. Does it seem clear to you that we are composed of soul and body? When all agreed, Navigius replied that he did not know. To whom I said: Do you know nothing at all, I ask, or is this to be counted among the things you do not know? I do not think I know everything, he said. Can you, I said, tell us something of what you know? I can, he said. If it is not troublesome, I said, please say something. And when he hesitated: Do you know, I said, at least that you are alive? I know, he said. Therefore you know you have life, since no one can live without life. And this, he said, I know. Do you also know that you have a body? He agreed. Therefore, you now know that you consist of body and life. I know in the meantime; but whether these alone are sufficient, I am uncertain. Therefore, you do not doubt that these two are body and soul; but you are uncertain whether there is something else that is capable of completing and perfecting a person. Thus, he said. What that might be, we will seek at another time, if we can, I said. Now I ask this

from all, since we all admit that a person cannot exist without body or soul, for what reason do we desire food? For the body, said Licentius. However, the others hesitated and discussed among themselves how food could seem necessary for the body, when it was desired for life, and life pertains only to the soul. Then I said: Does it seem to you that food pertains to that part which we see growing stronger by food? They agreed except for Trygetius. For he said: Why then did I not grow because of my gluttony? Everything has its limit set by nature, I said, beyond which it cannot progress: however, that limit would be smaller if they were deprived of food; which we notice more easily in livestock. And no one doubts that when food is removed, the bodies of all living beings grow thin. "To grow thin," said Licentius, "not to decrease." That is enough for me, I said, for what I want. For the question is whether food pertains to the body. It does pertain, since when it is taken away, it leads to thinness. Thus, they all concluded.

8. What then about the soul, I said? Does it have no proper food? Or does its food seem to you to be knowledge? Certainly, said the mother; I believe the soul has no other nourishment than the understanding of things and knowledge. When Trygetius showed himself doubtful about this opinion, she said: Today, did you not teach yourself from where or where the soul is nourished? For after a part of the meal, you said you did not notice which vessel we were using, because you were thinking about some other things I do not know, yet you did not refrain your hands and bites from the food itself. Where then was your mind, at the time when it did not pay attention while you were eating that? Believe me, from such feasts the mind is nourished, that is, from its theories and thoughts, if through them it can perceive something. When they were hesitating about this matter: Do you not concede, I said, that the minds of the most learned men are much fuller and greater than those of the unlearned? They said it was evident. Therefore, we rightly say that the minds of those who have been educated in no disciplines and have drawn nothing from the good arts

are hungry and almost famished. "Full," said Trygetius, "I think their minds are, but with vices and wickedness." That very thing is, I said, believe me, a certain sterility and almost famine of souls. For just as the body, when food is removed, is often filled with diseases and scabs, which indicate hunger; so their minds are full of diseases that confess their own hunger. Indeed, wickedness itself, the mother of all vices, because it is in vain, that is, because it is nothing, the ancients wanted to call it so. To which vice the contrary virtue is called frugality. Thus, this is named from fruitfulness, that is, from fruit, for the sake of a certain fertility of souls; so that one is named from sterility, that is, from nothing, wickedness: for nothing is everything that flows, that dissolves, that liquefies and almost always perishes. Therefore, we call such men lost. However, something is if it remains, if it is consistent, if it is always such as virtue, of which a great part is and the most beautiful, which is called temperance and frugality. But if this is more obscure than that you can now see it; certainly you concede that if even the minds of the unlearned are full, as the bodies, then two kinds of nourishment are found in souls; one healthy and useful, the other morbid and pestilential.

9. Since these things are so, I think on my birthday, since it is agreed among us that there are two certain things in man, namely body and soul, I ought to provide not only a somewhat more sumptuous meal for our bodies but also for our souls. But what this meal is, if you are hungry, I will present. For if I attempt to nourish you unwilling and disdainful, I will waste my effort; and rather prayers should be made, that you desire such feasts rather than those of the body. This will happen if your minds are healthy: for the sick, as we see in the diseases of the body itself, refuse and reject their food. They all said with their very faces and agreeing voices that they wanted to take and devour whatever I had prepared.

10. And I, starting again: Do we wish to be blessed, I ask? Hardly had I uttered this, when they all agreed in one voice. Do you think, I ask,

that a person is blessed who does not have what he wants? They denied it. What? Is everyone who has what he wants blessed? Then the mother: If he wants and has good things, he is blessed; but if he wants bad things, even if he has them, he is miserable. To which I, smiling and eager: Indeed, mother, you have truly grasped the essence of philosophy. For without a doubt, you have run out of words, so that you do not expose yourself as Tully just did, whose words on this sentiment are these. For in the work on the praise and defense of philosophy by Hortensius: "Behold," he says, "not philosophers indeed, but still eager to debate, all say that those who live as they wish are blessed." That is indeed false: For wanting what is not fitting is itself the most wretched. Nor is it so miserable not to attain what you want, as it is to attain what you should not want. For the wickedness of the will brings more harm than fortune does to anyone's good. In these words, she exclaimed in such a way that, having entirely forgotten her gender, we believed that some great man was sitting with us, while I, as much as I could, understood from where she spoke, and how they flowed from a divine source. And Licentius: But you must say, he says, that for someone to be blessed, he must know what he ought to want, and what things he ought to desire to have. Invite me, I say, to your birthday, whenever you deem it worthy; whatever you provide, I will gladly accept. With this condition, I ask that you feast with me today, nor demand what perhaps is not prepared. When she regretted her modest and shy reminder: Therefore, I say, it is agreed between us, that no one can be blessed who does not have what he wants; nor can everyone who has what he wants be blessed? They agreed.

11. What do you concede, I ask, that everyone who is not blessed is miserable? They did not hesitate. Therefore, I say, everyone who does not have what he wants is miserable. This pleased all. What then should a person acquire to be blessed, I ask? Perhaps this will also be provided in our banquet, lest Licentius's greed be neglected: for I think he must acquire what he has when he wants it. They said it is evident.

Therefore, I say, this must always remain, not dependent on fortune, nor subject to any circumstances. For whatever is mortal and fleeting cannot be possessed by us whenever we want and as long as we want. They all agreed. But Trygetius: There are, he says, many fortunate people who possess those very fragile things subject to chance, yet joyfully possess them abundantly for this life, and lack nothing of what they want. To which I replied: Do you think that a person who fears can be blessed? He does not seem so, he says. Therefore, if someone loves something and can lose it, can he not fear? He cannot, he says. However, those fortuitous things can be lost. Therefore, whoever loves and possesses these cannot in any way be blessed. No one objected. However, at this point, the mother: Even if he is secure, she says, that he will not lose all these things, still he cannot be satisfied with such things. Therefore, he is miserable in that he is always in need. To which I said: What if someone, overflowing with all these things and abounding, sets a limit to his desires, and decently and joyfully enjoys them; does it not seem to you that he is blessed? Not therefore, he says, is he blessed by those things, but by the moderation of his own mind. Excellent, I say, neither should anything else be answered to this question, nor should anything else be said by you. Therefore, we do not doubt at all, if someone decides to be blessed, that he must acquire what always remains, which cannot be taken away by any raging fortune. This, says Trygetius, we have long since agreed upon. Does God, I say, seem to you eternal and always remaining? Indeed, says Licentius, it is so certain that it needs no questioning; and all the others sang in pious devotion. Therefore, I say, whoever has God is blessed.

12. When they received this with great joy: Therefore, I say, I think we need to seek nothing else, except whether any man has God; for surely he will be blessed. About whom I ask what seems to you. Here Licentius: He has God who lives well. Trygetius: He has God, he says, who does what God wishes to be done. Lastidianus agreed with this sentiment. But that youngest boy of all: He has God, he says, who does

not have an unclean spirit. The mother, however, approved of everything, but especially this. Navigius was silent. When I asked him what he thought, he replied that he liked that last point. Nor did it seem right to neglect asking Rusticus what his opinion was on such a significant matter, who appeared to me to be silenced more by shame than by deliberation; he agreed with Trygetius.

13. Then I said: I hold all the opinions on this truly great matter, and beyond which nothing ought to be sought, nor can it be found, if only we investigate it as we began, most serenely and sincerely. Because today it is long, and they have a certain luxury in their feasts, if they rush into them excessively and voraciously (for in this way they digest badly in some manner; hence, one must be wary of the health of the minds no less than from that very hunger), it will be better for us to receive this question tomorrow when we are hungry, if it seems right. I just want to mention something that suddenly came to my mind to be brought forth by your servant; and it is, unless I am mistaken, such as is usually served last, as if prepared and seasoned with scholastic honey. Upon hearing this, they all leaned forward as if to an exalted dish, and urged me to hasten to say what it was. What, I say, do you think, except that the whole matter we undertook has been completed with the Academics? Upon receiving this name, those three who knew the matter rose more cheerfully; and as if extending their hands, as is customary, they assisted the servant bringing it in, showing with whatever words they could that they would hear nothing more delightful.

14. Thus I proposed the matter. If it is evident, I say, that a person is not blessed who does not have what he wants, which reason demonstrated a little while ago; no one seeks what he does not want to find, and those who always seek the truth: they therefore want to find; they want therefore to have the discovery of the truth. But they do not find: it follows that they do not have what they want; and from this it also

follows that they are not blessed. But no wise person is, unless blessed: therefore the Academic is not wise. Suddenly they all exclaimed, as if seizing the whole thing. But Licentius, more attentively and cautiously considering, feared agreement, and said: Indeed, I was carried away with you, since I exclaimed, moved by that conclusion. But I will admit nothing into my innards from here, and I will keep my part for Alypius: for either he will lick it with me, or he will remind me why it should not be touched. Sweet things, I say, should be feared more by Navigius, with a vicious spleen. Here he, smiling: Indeed, he says, such things will heal me. For I do not know how this twisted and prickly thing, which you placed, as he says, from Hymettus honey, is sharply sweet, and does not inflate the innards at all. Therefore, even though I somewhat gnaw at it with my palate, I still gladly throw it into my marrow as much as I can. For I do not see how this conclusion can be refuted. It cannot be refuted in any way, says Trygetius. Therefore, I have long rejoiced that I have taken on enmities with them. For I do not know by what urging nature, or, to speak more truly, God, even without knowing how they should be refuted, I was nevertheless very much opposed to them.

15. Here Licentius: I do not yet abandon them. Therefore, says Trygetius, do you dissent from us? Do you, he says, dissent from Alypius? To whom I said: I do not doubt, I say, that if Alypius were present, he would yield to this reasoning. For he could not think so absurdly, that either that blessed person would seem to be one who does not have that greatest good of the mind, which he ardently wishes to have, or that they do not want to find the truth, or that someone who is not blessed could be wise: for these three, as if from honey, flour, and nuts, that which you fear to taste is composed. Would he, he says, yield to such a small temptation of children, having abandoned such great abundance of the Academics, which, flooding this, I do not know what, would either be buried or dragged away? As if, I say, we were seeking something long, especially against Alypius: for these lit-

tle things being not moderately small are strong and useful, he would argue sufficiently for himself from his own body. But you, who chose to depend on the authority of the absent, which of these do you not approve? Whether it is that a person is not blessed who does not have what he wants? Or do you deny that they want to have the discovered truth, which they seek vehemently? Or do you think that anyone wise is not blessed? He is indeed blessed, he says, who does not have what he wants, as if smiling in a fit of anger. When I ordered this to be written down: I did not say, he says, exclaiming. When I also nodded for it to be written: I said, he says. And I had once commanded that no word be uttered except for the letters. Thus I held the young man agitated between modesty and firmness.

16. But when I jokingly addressed him with these words, as if we were provoking him to partake of his portion, I noticed that the others were ignorant of the whole matter, but wanting to know what was being discussed so pleasantly among us alone, gazing at us without laughter. They seemed to me to be completely similar, as often happens, to those who, when they feast among the most eager and greedy guests, either abstain from seizing or are deterred by shame. And because I had invited, and the person of a certain great man, and to explain it all, I was also bearing the inviter of a true man in that feast, I could not endure, and that inequality of our table and discrepancy moved me. I smiled at the mother. And she, very freely commanding that what they had less of should be brought forth as if from her own storeroom: Now tell us, she says, and reveal who these Academics are, and what they want? To whom I briefly explained openly, so that none of them would depart ignorant: These men, he says, are the fallible ones (by which name they are commonly called among us, whom the comitial disease subverts), and he rose up at once to leave; and here we all, happy and laughing, departed, with a boundary having been interposed.

3

CHAPTER THREE

Disputation of the second day. *Who has God in such a way that he is blessed? An unclean spirit is usually called in two ways.*

17. The next day, however, when we had again sat down after dinner, but somewhat later than the previous day, I said: You have come late to the banquet: which I think has happened not because of a lack of food, but because of the security of the few dishes; for it did not seem that it should be approached so early, since you thought you would perish quickly. For indeed, it was not to be believed that much remained, where so little had been found on the very day and solemnity. Perhaps rightly. But what has been prepared for you, I also do not know with you. For there is another who, with all, especially provides such feasts; but we often cease from eating, either from weakness, or satiety, or business: who, remaining among men, it was agreed among us yesterday, if I am not mistaken, to make them blessed piously and steadfastly. For when reason had demonstrated that he is blessed who has God, and no one of you had opposed this opinion, it was asked who seemed to you to have God. Concerning this matter, if I remember correctly, three opinions were stated. For part of the group agreed that he has God who does those things which God wants. However, some said that he has God who lives well. To the rest, however, God

seemed to be in those things in which the one called unclean spirit is not.

18. But perhaps you all felt the same one thing with different words. For if we consider the first two, every man who lives well does those things which God wants; and every man who does those things which God wants lives well; and there is nothing else to live well than to do those things which please God: unless something else seems to you. They agreed. However, that third must be considered a little more diligently, because, as I understand, the unclean spirit is usually called in two ways by the most chaste rites of sacred things: either he who invades the soul from outside and disturbs the senses, and inflicts a certain madness on men; to whom those who are in charge are said to impose hands or to exorcise, that is, to expel him by divine adjuration: otherwise, however, the unclean spirit is said to be every completely unclean soul; which is nothing other than polluted by vices and errors. Therefore, I ask you, boy, who perhaps with a somewhat clearer and purer spirit has expressed this opinion, who seems to you not to have the unclean spirit: he who does not have a demon, by which mad men are made; or he who has cleansed his soul from all vices and sins? He seems to me, he said, not to have the unclean spirit, who lives chastely. But chaste, I said, whom do you call? him who sins nothing, or him who only refrains from illicit intercourse? How, he said, can he be chaste, who, abstaining only from illicit intercourse, does not cease to be polluted by other sins? He is truly chaste, who attends to God and holds himself to Him alone. These words of the boy, as they were said, when it pleased me to be written down: Therefore, I said, it is necessary that he lives well, and he who lives well is necessarily such; unless something else seems to you. He conceded with the others. Therefore, here is one opinion stated, I said.

19. But I ask you this a little: does God will that man seeks God? They granted. Again I ask; can we say that he who seeks God lives

badly? In no way, they said. Also answer this third; can the unclean spirit seek God? They denied, with Navigius hesitating somewhat, who later yielded to the voices of the others. If therefore, I said, he who seeks God does what God wants, and lives well, and does not have the unclean spirit; but he who seeks God does not yet have God: therefore, not everyone who either lives well, or does what God wants, or does not have the unclean spirit, is to be believed to have God immediately. When the others laughed at their concessions, the mother, having been long stupid, requested that I explain and release what I had said, which was entangled by the necessity of the conclusion. When this had been done: But no one, he said, can come to God, unless he has sought God. Very well, I said. Yet he who still seeks has not yet reached God, even if he lives well. Therefore, not everyone who lives well has God. To me, he said, it seems that no one does not have God: but he who lives well has a propitious one; he who lives badly, a hostile one. Therefore, I said, yesterday we conceded that he is blessed who has God: since indeed every man has God, yet not every man is blessed. Therefore, add, he said, propitious.

20. At least, I said, this is sufficiently clear among us, that he is blessed who has a propitious God? I would like, he said, to agree: but I fear for him who still seeks; especially lest you conclude that the Academic is blessed, who yesterday in a common and poorly Latin speech, but certainly very apt, as it seems to me, was called a transient. For I cannot say that a man seeking God is against God: for if it is blasphemous to say, he will be propitious; and he who has a propitious God is blessed. Therefore, he will be blessed who seeks: however, every seeker does not yet have what he wants. Therefore, there will be a blessed man who does not have what he wants, which yesterday seemed absurd to all of us; whence we believed that the darkness of the Academics had been dispelled. Therefore, Licentius will now triumph over us; and to me those sweet things, which I recklessly accepted against

my health, will demand these penalties from me, as a wise doctor will admonish.

21. When the mother had also responded: "I," she said, "think differently; I do not immediately concede that God is opposed to one whom He does not favor, but I believe there is something in between." To which I said: "Do you concede that this man, I say, is in between, to whom neither God is favorable nor hostile, can in any way have God?" When he hesitated, the mother said: "It is one thing to have God, another not to be without God." I said: "What then is better; to have God, or not to be without God?" She replied: "As far as I can understand, this is my opinion: he who lives well has God, but favorable; he who lives poorly has God, but hostile. However, whoever still seeks and has not yet found, neither favorable nor hostile, is not without God." I said: "Is this also your opinion?" They said it was. "Tell me, please," I said: "does it not seem to you that God is favorable to the man whom He supports?" They confessed it was so. "Therefore," I said, "does God not support the man seeking Him?" They answered: "He supports." "Therefore," I said, "he who seeks God has a favorable God; and everyone who has a favorable God is blessed. Therefore, he who seeks is also blessed. However, he who seeks does not yet have what he wants. Therefore, will he be blessed who does not have what he wants?" "Indeed," said the mother, "it does not seem to me that he is blessed who does not have what he wants." "Therefore," I said, "not everyone who has a favorable God is blessed." "If reason thinks this," she said, "I cannot deny it." "Therefore," I said, "the distribution will be such that everyone who has found God and has a favorable God is blessed; however, everyone who seeks has a favorable God but is not yet blessed; indeed, whoever alienates himself from God by vices and sins is not only not blessed, but does not even live with God favorably."

22. When this pleased everyone: "Well then," I said; "but I still fear that it may trouble you that we previously conceded that whoever is not blessed is miserable: to whom it will follow to be a miserable man who holds a favorable God, whom we have not yet said to be blessed while still seeking God. Or indeed, as Cicero says, do we call the wealthy owners of many estates on earth; shall we name the possessors of all virtues as poor? But see this, whether it is true that every needy person is miserable, just as it is true that every miserable person is needy. For it will be true that there is nothing else that misery is but need, which you felt I was praising just now when it was said. However, it is long today to seek this; therefore, I ask that it not be a burden for you to gather at this table again tomorrow." When all had said they would gladly do so, we rose.

4

CHAPTER FOUR

Discussion of the third day. *Regarding the question proposed the day before, it must be said. Every person in need is miserable. Furthermore, a wise person is not in need of anything. Whether everyone who is miserable is in need. The need of the mind. The fullness of the mind. Who ultimately is blessed.*

23. The third day of our discussion, having dissipated the morning clouds that compelled us to the baths, rendered the afternoon time most bright. Therefore, it was pleasing to descend into the nearby meadow, and while it seemed convenient to all of us to sit down, the remaining conversation was carried out in this manner. Almost everything, I say, that I wanted to be conceded to me by you in response to my questioning, I have and hold: hence, on this day, which we can finally distinguish our gathering by some interval of days, there will be either nothing or not much, as I think, that you will need to respond to me. For it had been said by my mother that misery is nothing other than need, and it has been agreed among us that all who are in need are miserable. But whether all miserable people are also in need is a question, which we could not explain yesterday. However, if reason demonstrates that this is the case, it has been perfectly found who is blessed: for he will be the one who is not in need. For everyone who is

not miserable is blessed. Therefore, he is blessed who is free from need, if it is established that the need we speak of is the same as misery.

24. For what, says Trygetius? Can it not be concluded from this that every person who is not in need is blessed, since it is evident that everyone who is in need is miserable? For I remember that we conceded there is nothing intermediate between the miserable and the blessed. Is there anything, I say, that seems to you to be intermediate between the dead and the living? Is not every person either alive or dead? I admit, he says, that there is nothing intermediate here: but what is the point of that? Because, I say, I believe you also concede that everyone who has been buried for a year is dead. He did not deny it. What about everyone who has not been buried for a year, is he alive? No, he says, it follows. Therefore, I say, it does not follow that if everyone who is in need is miserable, then everyone who is not in need is blessed, although nothing can be found intermediate between the miserable and the blessed, as between the living and the dead.

25. When some of them understood this a little late, I opened it up to their understanding with words I could find that suited them: Therefore, I say, no one doubts that every person who is in need is miserable: nor are we frightened by certain necessities of the body for the wise. For the mind itself, in which the blessed life is placed, is not in need of them. For it is perfect; however, no perfect person is in need of anything: and what seems necessary for the body he will take, if it is present; if it is not present, the lack of those things will not break him. For every wise person is strong; however, no strong person fears anything. Therefore, the wise does not fear either the death of the body or the pains, for the avoidance or evasion or delay of which those things are necessary, of which he may be affected by lack. But nonetheless, he does not cease to use them well, if they are not lacking. For that saying is very true: For you to admit what you can avoid is foolishness. (Terence in Eunuchus, act 4, scene 6) Therefore, he will avoid death

and pain as much as he can and as much as is appropriate; so that if he does not avoid them at all, he is not miserable because these things happen, but because he did not want to avoid them when he could: which is a clear sign of folly. Therefore, one who does not avoid these things will be miserable, not by the experience of those things, but by folly. But if he was unable to avoid them, when he acted diligently and appropriately, those things falling upon him will not make him miserable. Indeed, that saying of the same comic is no less true: Since what you want cannot happen, wish for what can. (Id. in Andria, act 2, scene 1.) How will he be miserable, to whom nothing happens except by his own will? Because what he sees cannot come to pass, he cannot will. For he has the will of the most certain things, that is, whatever he does, he does not act except according to a certain prescription of virtue and the divine law of wisdom, which can in no way be taken from him.

26. Now see whether every miserable person is in need. For the difficulty of conceding to this opinion is caused by the fact that many are established in a great abundance of fortunate things, to whom all things are so easy that whatever desire asks is at their beck and call. Indeed, this life is difficult. But let us imagine someone like the one whom Cicero says was Oratus. For who can easily say that Oratus suffered from need, a very wealthy man, most charming, most delightful, who lacked nothing for pleasure, nor for favor, nor for good and sound health? For he abounded in most profitable estates and most delightful friends, as much as he wished; and he used all those things most suitably for the health of his body, and (to briefly explain it all) his entire plan and will was followed by prosperous success. But perhaps someone among you is disturbed, thinking that he wished to have more than he had. We do not know this. But what is sufficient for the question, let us make him not desiring more than he held. Do you see him as lacking? Even if I concede, says Licentius, that he desired nothing, which I do not know how to take in a non-wise man; he neverthe-

less feared, for he was a man, as it is said, of no bad intellect, that all those things might be snatched from him by some adverse blow. For it was not difficult to understand that all such things, however great they were, were established under circumstances. Then I, smiling, said: You see, Licentius, that most fortunate man hindered from a blessed life by the goodness of his intellect. For the sharper he was, the more he saw that he could lose all those things; the more he was broken by fear, and he asserted that common saying: An unfaithful man is wise in his own misfortune.

27. Here, when both he and the others had smiled: However, I say, let us pay closer attention to this, because even if this man was afraid, he did not lack: hence the question arises. To lack is to not have, not to fear losing what you have. However, this man was wretched because he was afraid, even though he did not lack. Therefore, not everyone who is wretched lacks. When he had approved this, along with the others, even though I was defending the opinion of someone, he still hesitated a bit: "I do not know," he said, "yet I do not fully understand how misery can be separated from lack, or lack from misery." For this man, who was rich and wealthy, and desired nothing more, as you say; yet because he was afraid of losing it, he lacked wisdom. Would we then say that this man is lacking if he lacked silver and money; when he lacked wisdom, would we not say so? When everyone exclaimed in wonder, I myself was also not a little cheerful and happy, because it had been said especially that which I had prepared to present as great from the books of philosophers, and lastly: "Do you see," I said, "that there is a difference between many various doctrines and a mind most attentive to God? For from where do those things we marvel at proceed, if not from there?" Here Licentius, joyfully exclaiming: "Absolutely," he said, "nothing truer, nothing more divine could be said. For there is no greater and more miserable lack than to lack wisdom; and he who does not lack wisdom cannot lack anything at all."

28. Therefore, I say, the lack of the mind is nothing other than folly. For this is contrary to wisdom, and so contrary as death is to life, as a blessed life is to a miserable one; this is, without any middle. For just as every non-blessed man is wretched, and every man who is not dead lives; so it is manifest that every non-foolish man is wise. From this, it is now permissible to see that Sergius Orata was not wretched merely because he feared he might lose the gifts of fortune, but because he was foolish. Hence, it follows that he would be more miserable if he had feared nothing at all with those things he thought were good, which were wavering and uncertain. For he would not be vigilant with fortitude, but more secure in the sleep of the mind, and submerged in a deeper folly. But if everyone who lacks wisdom suffers great poverty, and everyone composed of wisdom lacks nothing, it follows that folly is lack. Just as every fool is wretched, so every wretched person is foolish. Therefore, just as every lack is misery, so every misery is proved to be lack.

29. When Trygetius said that he understood this conclusion poorly: "What," I said, "is the reasoning that agrees among us? He lacks," he said, "who does not have wisdom. What is, therefore," I said, "to lack? Not to have wisdom," he said. "What is," I said, "not to have wisdom?" Here, when he was silent, is this not, I said, to have folly? "This," he said. Therefore, there is nothing else, I said, to have lack than folly; from which it is now necessary that lack be named by another word when folly is named. Although I do not know how we should say, "He has lack," or, "he has folly." For it is as if we say a certain place, which lacks light, has darkness: which is nothing other than not having light. For darkness does not come or recede; but to lack light is to be dark, just as to lack clothing is to be naked. For nakedness does not flee as some movable thing approaches. Thus, we say someone has lack, as if we say he has nakedness. For lack is a word for not having. Therefore, in order to explain what I want as best as I can, it is said, "He has lack"; as if it were said, "He has not having." Therefore, if it has been

shown that folly itself is true and certain lack, see now the question we have undertaken, whether it is resolved. For it was doubted among us whether when we called misery, we named nothing other than lack. However, we have given a reason that folly is rightly called lack. Just as therefore every fool is wretched, and every wretched person is foolish; so it is necessary to admit that not only every person who lacks is wretched, but also that every person who is wretched is lacking. But if from the fact that every fool is wretched, and every wretched person is foolish, it follows that folly is misery; why do we not conclude from the fact that whoever lacks is wretched, and whoever is wretched lacks, that nothing else is misery than lack?

30. When everyone admitted that it was so: "It follows now," I said, "that we see who does not lack; for he will be wise and blessed. However, lack is folly, and the name of lack: this word, however, usually signifies a certain sterility and poverty. Please pay attention more deeply, how great the care of ancient men, whether everything or, as is evident, certain words were created, of those things especially of which knowledge was most necessary. For now you concede that every fool lacks, and that everyone who lacks is foolish: I believe you also concede that a foolish mind is vicious, and that all vices of the mind are included under one name of folly. However, on the first day of this discussion of ours, we had said that wickedness was named from that which is nothing, of which the contrary frugality was named from grain. Therefore, in those two opposites, namely frugality and wickedness, those two seem to stand out, being and not being. But what do we think is contrary to the lack about which the question is? Here, when they hesitated a bit: "If I say," said Trygetius, "riches; I see that poverty is contrary to these." Indeed, I said, it is nearby. For poverty and lack are usually taken as one and the same. Nevertheless, another word must be found, lest the better part lack a single term, so that when that part abounds with the name of poverty and lack, from this side only the name of riches is opposed. For nothing is more absurd

than that there is a lack of the word here, where there is a contrary part to lack. "Plenitude," said Licentius, "if it can be said, seems to me to be rightly opposed to lack."

31. Later, I say, we shall perhaps inquire more diligently about the word. For this is not to be cared for in the investigation of truth. Although the most excellent Sallust, a careful weigh of words, opposed wealth to poverty (Sallust, On the Catiline War); nevertheless, I accept that fullness. For we shall not labor here under the fear of grammarians, nor should we fear being chastised by them for using words carelessly, those who have given us their things to use. When they had agreed: Therefore, because your minds, I say, are intent on God, I have decided not to despise them as certain oracles, let us see what this name means; for I think there is none more suitable for truth. Therefore, fullness and poverty are contrary: but also here, just as in wickedness and frugality, those two appear, to be and not to be. And if poverty itself is foolishness, then fullness will be wisdom. Many have rightly said that frugality is the mother of all virtues. Agreeing with them, Cicero also says in a popular speech: Let each one receive as he wishes; yet I judge frugality, that is modesty and temperance, to be the greatest virtue (Speech for Dejotarus). Certainly very learnedly and appropriately: for he considered frugality, that is, that which we say is being, of which not being is contrary. But because of the common custom of speaking, where frugality is usually said to be like thriftiness, he illustrated what he sensed by two subsequent words, subjecting modesty and temperance: and let us pay more careful attention to these two words.

32. Modesty is certainly derived from measure, and temperance from temper. Where there is measure and temper, there is neither more nor less. Therefore, it is fullness itself, which we had set against poverty, much better than if we had placed abundance. For in abundance, affluence and a sort of overflowing of something excessively ex-

uberant are understood. When this occurs beyond what is sufficient, there is also a need for measure, and that which is excessive needs moderation. Therefore, poverty is not alien from excess itself; from measure, however, both more and less are alien. If you also scrutinize wealth, you will find that it holds nothing other than measure. For wealth is said to be from abundance. But how does that which is excessive help, when it is often more inconvenient than too little? Therefore, whatever is either too little or too much, because it needs measure, is subject to poverty. Therefore, the measure of the mind is wisdom. Indeed, wisdom is not denied to be contrary to foolishness, and foolishness is poverty, but fullness is contrary to poverty. Therefore, wisdom is fullness. In fullness, however, there is measure. Therefore, the measure of the mind is in wisdom. Hence, that is noteworthy, and not without reason is it said to be the first useful thing in life: Not to exceed anything. (Terence in Andria, Act 1, Scene 1.)

33. However, we had said at the beginning of our discussion today that if we found nothing else to be misery than poverty, we would admit that he is blessed who does not suffer want. But it has been discovered: therefore, to be blessed is nothing other than not to suffer want, that is, to be wise. If, however, you ask what wisdom is (for reason has also developed and extracted it as much as it could at present); it is nothing other than the measure of the mind, that is, by which the mind balances itself, so that it neither rushes into excess nor is constrained below what is full. It rushes into luxuries, dominations, pride, and other such things, by which the immoderate think that they acquire joys and powers for themselves. However, it is constrained by filth, fears, sorrow, desire, and other things, whatever they are, by which even miserable men confess to be miserable. But when it contemplates wisdom found, and when, to use the word of this boy, it holds itself to it, and does not turn to the deception of simulacra, the weight of which is accustomed to fall and sink from its God, it is not moved by any emptiness; it fears nothing of immoderation, and

therefore nothing of poverty, nothing, therefore, of misery. Therefore, whoever is blessed has his measure, that is, wisdom.

34. But what is to be said of wisdom, if not that which is the Wisdom of God? We have also received from divine authority that the Son of God is nothing other than the Wisdom of God (1 Corinthians 1:24): and the Son of God is indeed God. Therefore, whoever is blessed has God: which has already pleased all of us, when we entered this banquet. But what do you think wisdom is, if not truth? For it has also been said: I am the Truth (John 14:6). However, for truth to be, it comes to be through some highest measure, from which it proceeds, and in which it perfectly turns. However, to that highest measure, no other measure is imposed: for if the highest measure is by the highest measure, it is by itself a measure. But also the highest measure must necessarily be a true measure. Therefore, just as truth is generated by measure, so measure is known by truth. Therefore, neither is truth without measure, nor has measure ever been without truth. Who is the Son of God? It has been said, Truth. Who is he who has no father, who other than the highest measure? Therefore, whoever comes to the highest measure through truth is blessed. This is to have God in the mind, that is, to enjoy God. For whatever is had from God, does not have God.

35. However, a certain admonition, which engages with us, urges us to remember God, to seek Him, to thirst for Him, casting aside all disdain, emanates from the very source of truth. This secret sun pours forth its light into our inner eyes. All that we speak is true, even when we boldly turn to it with eyes that are still less healthy or suddenly opened, and we tremble to behold it in its entirety: and nothing else appears to be this than God, perfect without any hindrance of degeneration. For there, all and everything is perfect, and at the same time, there is the most omnipotent God. Yet, as long as we seek, we have not yet reached the very source, and to use that word, we

have not yet been filled to our measure: and therefore, although with God's help we are already seeking, we are not yet wise and blessed. Thus, that is the fullness of the satisfaction of souls, this is the blessed life, to know piously and perfectly from whom you are led into the truth, by which truth you may enjoy, through which you may be connected in the highest way. These three show one God to those who understand, and one substance, excluding the vanities of various superstitions. Here, the mother, recognizing the words that were deeply rooted in her memory, and as if awakening in her faith, poured forth that verse of our priest: "Nurture the praying ones, Trinity," (Ambrose in hymn, God creator of all.) and added: "This is the blessed life without any doubt, which is the perfect life, to which we must hasten to be led, with solid faith, cheerful hope, and blazing charity."

36. Therefore, I say, since the very manner admonishes us to distinguish the banquet by some interval of days, I give thanks to the highest and true God the Father, the Lord liberator of souls, as much as I can for my efforts; then to you who have been invited in harmony, and who have also enriched me with many gifts. For you have contributed so much to our conversation that I cannot deny being satisfied by my invited guests. Here, all rejoicing and praising God: "How I wish," says Trygetius, "that you would nourish us this way every day."

LATIN TEXT

CAPUT PRIMUM.-- *Praefatio. Dicat librum Theodoro, eique aperit quibus veluti ventis ad christianae philosophiae portum impulsus sit. Occasio disputationis.*

1. Si ad philosophiae portum, de quo jam in beatae vitae regionem solumque proceditur, vir humanissime atque magne, Theodore, ratione institutus cursus, et voluntas ipsa perduceret; nescio utrum temere dixerim, multo minoris numeri homines ad eum perventuros fuisse, quamvis nunc quoque, ut videmus, rari admodum paucique perveniant. Cum enim in hunc mundum, sive Deus, sive natura, sive necessitas, sive voluntas nostra, sive conjuncta horum aliqua, sive simul omnia (res enim multum obscura est, sed tamen a te jam illustranda suscepta) veluti in quoddam procellosum salum nos quasi temere passimque projecerit; quotusquisque cognosceret quo sibi nitendum esset, quave redeundum, nisi aliquando et invitos contraque obnitentes aliqua tempestas, quae stultis videtur adversa, in optatissimam terram nescientes errantesque compingeret?

2. Igitur hominum quos philosophia potest accipere, tria quasi navigantium genera mihi videor videre. Unum est eorum, quos ubi aetas compos rationis assumpserit, parvo impetu pulsuque remorum de proximo fugiunt, seseque condunt in illa tranquillitate, unde caeteris civibus quibus possunt, quo admoniti conentur ad se, lucidissimum signum sui alicujus operis erigunt. Alterum vero est eorum, superiorique contrarium, qui fallacissima facie maris decepti, elegerunt in medium progredi, longeque a sua patria peregrinari audent, et saepe ejus obliviscuntur. Hos si nescio quo et nimis latente modo a puppi ventus, quem prosperum putant, fuerit prosecutus, penetrant in altissima miseriarum elati atque gaudentes, quod eis usquequaque fallacissima serenitas voluptatum honorumque blanditur. His profecto quid aliud optandum est, quam quaedam in illis rebus a quibus jacti

excipiuntur, improspera; et, si parum est, saeviens omnino tempestas, contrarieque flans ventus, qui eos ad certa et solida gaudia, vel flentes gementesque perducat? hujus generis tamen plerique nondum longius evagati, quibusdam non ita gravibus molestiis reducuntur. Hi sunt homines, quos cum vel lacrymabiles tragoediae fortunarum suarum, vel inanium negotiorum anxiae difficultates, quasi nihil aliud habentes quod agant, in libros doctorum sapientissimorumque hominum truserint, in ipso quodammodo portu evigilant, unde illos nulla maris illius promissa nimium falso ridentis excludant. Est autem genus inter haec tertium eorum, qui vel in ipso adolescentiae limine, vel jam diu multumque jactati, tamen quaedam signa respiciunt, et suae dulcissimae patriae, quamvis in ipsis fluctibus recordantur: et aut recto cursu in nullo falsi, et nihil morati, eam repetunt; aut plerumque vel inter nubila deviantes, vel mergentia contuentes sidera, vel nonnullis illecebris capti, bonae navigationis tempora differentes, errant diutius, saepe etiam periclitantur. Quos item saepe nonnulla in fluxis fortunis calamitas, quasi conatibus eorum adversa tempestas, in optatissimam patriam quietamque compellit.

3. His autem omnibus, qui quocumque modo ad beatae vitae regionem feruntur, unus immanissimus mons ante ipsum portum constitutus, qui etiam magnas ingredientibus gignit angustias, vehementissime formidandus, cautissimeque vitandus est. Nam ita fulget, ita mentiente illa luce vestitur, ut non solum pervenientibus, nondumque ingressis incolendum se offerat, et eorum voluntatibus pro ipsa beata terra satisfacturum polliceatur; sed plerumque de ipso portu ad sese homines invitat, eosque nonnunquam detinet ipsa altitudine delectatos, unde caeteros despicere libeat. Hi tamen admonent saepe venientes, ne aut occultis subter scopulis decipiantur, aut ad se ascendere facile putent; et qua sine periculo ingrediantur propter illius terrae vicinitatem, benevolentissime docent. Ita cum eis invident vanissimam gloriam, locum securitatis ostendunt. Nam quem montem alium vult intelligi ratio propinquantibus ad philosophiam ingressisve metuendum, nisi superbum studium inanissimae gloriae, quod ita nihil intus plenum atque solidum habet, ut inflatos sibi superambu-

lantes succrepante fragili solo demergat ac sorbeat, eisque in tenebras revolutis, eripiat luculentissimam domum, quam pene jam viderant?

4. Quae cum ita sint, accipe, mi Theodore, namque ad id quod desidero, te unum intueor, teque aptissimum semper admiror; accipe, inquam, et quod illorum trium genus hominum me tibi dederit, et quo loco mihi esse videar, et abs te cujusmodi auxilium certus exspectem. Ego ab usque undevigesimo anno aetatis meae, postquam in schola rhetoris librum illum Ciceronis, qui Hortensius vocatur, accepi, tanto amore philosophiae succensus sum, ut statim ad eam me transferre meditarer. Sed neque mihi nebulae defuerunt, quibus confunderetur cursus meus; et diu, fateor, quibus in errorem ducebar, labentia in oceanum astra suspexi. Nam et superstitio quaedam puerilis me ab ipsa inquisitione terrebat: et ubi factus erectior, illam caliginem dispuli, mihique persuasi docentibus potius quam jubentibus esse credendum; incidi in homines quibus lux ista quae oculis cernitur, inter summa et divina colenda videretur. Non assentiebar, sed putabam eos magnum aliquid tegere illis involucris, quod essent aliquando aperturi. At ubi discussos eos evasi, maxime trajecto isto mari, diu gubernacula mea repugnantia omnibus ventis in mediis fluctibus Academici tenuerunt. Deinde veni in has terras; hic septentrionem cui me crederem didici. Animadverti enim et saepe in sacerdotis nostri, et aliquando in sermonibus tuis, cum de Deo cogitaretur, nihil omnino corporis esse cogitandum, neque cum de anima: nam id est unum in rebus proximum Deo. Sed ne in philosophiae gremium celeriter advolarem, fateor, uxoris honorisque illecebra detinebar; ut cum haec essem consecutus, tum demum me, quod paucis felicissimis licuit, totis velis omnibusque remis in illum sinum raperem, ibique conquiescerem. Lectis autem Platonis paucissimis libris, cujus te esse studiosissimum accepi, collataque cum eis, quantum potui, etiam illorum auctoritate qui divina mysteria tradiderunt, sic exarsi, ut omnes illas vellem anchoras rumpere, nisi me nonnullorum hominum existimatio commoveret (Conf. lib. 7, capp. 9, 20). Quid ergo restabat aliud, nisi ut immoranti mihi superfluis, tempestas quae putabatur adversa, succurreret? Itaque tantus me arripuit pectoris dolor, ut illius profes-

sionis onus sustinere non valens, qua mihi velificabam fortasse ad Sirenas, abjicerem omnia, et optatae tranquillitati vel quassatam navem fissamque perducerem.

5. Ergo vides in qua philosophia quasi in portu navigem. Sed etiam ipse late patet, ejusque magnitudo quamvis jam minus periculosum, non tamen penitus excludit errorem. Nam cui parti terrae, quae profecto una beata est, me admoveam, atque contingam, prorsus ignoro. Quid enim solidum tenui, cui adhuc de anima quaestio nutat et fluctuat? Quare obsecro te per virtutem tuam, per humanitatem, per animarum inter se vinculum atque commercium, ut dexteram porrigas. Hoc autem est, ut me ames, et a me vicissim te amari credas charumque haberi. Quod si impetravero, ad ipsam beatam vitam, cui te jam haerere praesumo, parvo conatu facillime accedam. Quid autem agam, quove modo ad istum portum necessarios meos congregem ut cognoscas, et ex eo animum meum (neque enim alia signa invenio quibus me ostendam) ut plenius intelligas, initium disputationum mearum, quod mihi videtur religiosius evasisse, atque tuo titulo dignius, ad te scribendum putavi, et ipso tuo nomine dedicandum. Aptissime sane; nam de beata vita quaesivimus inter nos, nihilque aliud video quod magis Dei donum vocandum sit. Eloquentia tua territus non sum; quidquid enim amo, quamvis non assequar, timere non possum: fortunae vero sublimitatem multo minus; apud te enim vere, quamvis sit magna, secunda est; nam quibus dominatur, eosdem ipsos secundos facit. Sed jam quid afferam, quaeso te, attende.

6. Idibus novembris mihi natalis dies erat: post tam tenue prandium, ut ab eo nihil ingeniorum impediretur, omnes qui simul non modo illo die, sed quotidie convivabamur, in balneas ad consedendum vocavi; nam is tempori aptus locus secretusque occurrerat. Erant autem, non enim vereor eos singulari benignitati tuae notos interim nominibus facere, in primis nostra mater, cujus meriti credo esse omne quod vivo; Navigius frater meus, Trygetius et Licentius, cives et discipuli mei; nec Lastidianum et Rusticum consobrinos meos, quamvis nullum vel grammaticum passi sint, deesse volui, ipsumque eorum sensum communem, ad rem quam moliebar, necessar-

ium putavi. Erat etiam nobiscum aetate minimus omnium, sed cujus ingenium, si amore non fallor, magnum quiddam pollicetur, Adeodatus filius meus. Quibus attentis, sic coepi.

CAPUT II.-- *Disputatio primae diei. Ex anima et corpore constamus. Cibus corpori necessarius. Animae quoque suus est cibus. Beatus non est qui quod vult non habet. Nec tamen omnis qui quod vult habet, beatus est. Quid sibi homo comparare debet ut sit beatus. Quis Deum habeat. Academicus beatus esse non potest, ergo nec sapiens.*

7. Manifestum vobis videtur ex anima et corpore nos esse compositos? Cum omnes consentirent, Navigius se ignorare respondit. Cui ego: Nihil, nihilne omnino scis, inquam, an inter aliqua quae ignoras etiam hoc numerandum est? Non puto me, inquit, omnia nescire. Potesne, inquam, nobis dicere aliquid eorum quae nosti? Possum, inquit. Nisi molestum est, inquam, profer aliquid. Et cum dubitaret: Scisne, inquam, saltem te vivere? Scio, inquit. Scis ergo habere te vitam, siquidem vivere nemo nisi vita potest. Et hoc, inquit, scio. Scis etiam corpus te habere? Assentiebatur. Ergo jam scis te constare ex corpore et vita. Scio interim; sed utrum haec sola sint, incertus sum. Ergo duo ista, inquam, esse non dubitas, corpus et animam; sed incertus es utrum sit aliud quod ad complendum ac perficiendum hominem valet. Ita, inquit. Hoc quale sit, alias, si possumus, quaeremus, inquam. Nunc illud jam ex omnibus quaero, cum fateamur cuncti neque sine corpore, neque sine anima esse posse hominem, cibos propter quid horum appetamus. Propter corpus, inquit Licentius. Caeteri autem cunctabantur, varioque sermone inter se agebant, quomodo posset propter corpus cibus necessarius videri, cum appeteretur propter vitam, et vita non nisi ad animam pertineret. Tum ego: Videtur, inquam, vobis ad eam partem cibum pertinere, quam cibo crescere robustioremque fieri videmus? Assentiebantur praeter Trygetium. Ait enim: Cur ergo non pro edacitate mea crevi? Modum, inquam, suum a natura constitutum habent omnia corpora, ultra quam mensuram progredi nequeant: tamen ea mensura minora essent, si eis alimenta defuissent; quod et in pecoribus facilius animadvertimus. Et nemo dubitat cibis subtractis

omnium animantium corpora macrescere. Macrescere, inquit Licentius, non decrescere. Satis est mihi, inquam, ad id quod volo. Etenim quaestio est utrum ad corpus cibus pertineat. Pertinet autem, cum eo subducto, ad maciem deducitur. Omnes ita esse censuerunt.

8. Quid ergo anima, inquam? nulla ne habet alimenta propria? an ejus esca scientia vobis videtur? Plane, inquit mater; nulla re alia credo ali animam quam intellectu rerum atque scientia. De qua sententia cum Trygetius dubium se ostenderet: hodie, inquit illa, tu ipse nonne docuisti unde aut ubi anima pascatur? Nam post aliquantam prandii partem te dixisti non advertisse quo vasculo uteremur, quod alia nescio quae cogitasses, nec tamen ab ipsa ciborum parte abstinueras manus atque morsus. Ubi igitur erat animus tuus, quo tempore illud, te vescente, non attendebat; inde, mihi crede, et talibus epulis animus pascitur, id est theoriis et cogitationibus suis, si per eas aliquid percipere possit. De qua re cum dubitanter streperent: Nonne, inquam, conceditis hominum doctissimorum animos multo esse quam imperitorum quasi in suo genere pleniores atque majores? Manifestum esse dixerunt. Recte igitur dicimus eorum animos, qui nullis disciplinis eruditi sunt, nihilque bonarum artium hauserunt, jejunos et quasi famelicos esse. Plenos, inquit Trygetius, et illorum animos esse arbitror, sed vitiis atque nequitia. Ista ipsa est, inquam, crede mihi, quaedam sterilitas et quasi fames animorum. Nam quemadmodum corpus detracto cibo plerumque morbis atque scabie repletur, quae in eo vitia indicant famem; ita et illorum animi pleni sunt morbis quibus sua jejunia confitentur. Etenim ipsam nequitiam matrem omnium vitiorum, ex eo quod nequidquam sit, id est ex eo quod nihil sit, veteres dictam esse voluerunt. Cui vitio quae contraria virtus est, frugalitas nominatur. Ut igitur haec a fruge, id est a fructu, propter quamdam animorum fecunditatem; ita illa ab sterilitate, hoc est a nihilo, nequitia nominata est: nihil est enim omne quod fluit, quod solvitur, quod liquescit et quasi semper perit. Ideo tales homines etiam perditos dicimus. Est autem aliquid, si manet, si constat, si semper tale est, ut est virtus, cujus magna pars est atque pulcherrima, quae temperantia et frugalitas dicitur. Sed si hoc obscurius est quam ut id jam vos

videre possitis; certe illud conceditis, quia si animi imperitorum etiam ipsi pleni sunt, ut corporum, ita animorum duo alimentorum genera inveniuntur; unum salubre atque utile, alterum morbidum atque pestiferum.

9. Quae cum ita sint, arbitror die natali meo, quoniam duo quaedam esse in homine convenit inter nos, id est corpus atque animam, non me prandium paulo lautius corporibus nostris solum, sed et animis etiam exhibere debere. Quod autem hoc sit prandium, si esuritis, proferam. Nam si vos invitos, et fastidientes alere conabor, frustra operam insumam; magisque vota facienda sunt, ut tales epulas potius quam illas corporis desideretis. Quod eveniet si sani animi vestri fuerint: aegri enim, sicut in morbis ipsius corporis videmus, cibos suos recusant et respuunt. Omnes se vultu ipso et consentiente voce, quidquid praeparassem jam sumere ac vorare velle dixerunt.

10. Atque ego rursus exordiens: Beatos esse nos volumus, inquam? Vix hoc effuderam, occurrerunt una voce consentientes. Videturne vobis, inquam, beatus esse qui quod vult non habet? Negaverunt. Quid? omnis qui quod vult habet, beatus est? Tum mater: Si bona, inquit, velit et habeat, beatus est; si autem mala velit, quamvis habeat, miser est. Cui ego arridens atque gestiens: Ipsam, inquam, prorsus, mater, arcem philosophiae tenuisti. Nam tibi procul dubio verba defuerunt, ut non sicut Tullius te modo panderes, cujus de hac sententia verba ista sunt. Nam in Hortensio, quem de laude ac defensione philosophiae librum fecit: Ecce autem, ait, non philosophi quidem, sed prompti tamen ad disputandum, omnes aiunt esse beatos qui vivant ut ipsi velint. Falsum id quidem: Velle enim quod non deceat, idem ipsum miserrimum. Nec tam miserum est non adipisci quod velis, quam adipisci velle quod non oporteat. Plus enim mali pravitas voluntatis affert, quam fortuna cuiquam boni. In quibus verbis illa sic exclamabat, ut obliti penitus sexus ejus, magnum aliquem virum considere nobiscum crederemus, me interim, quantum poteram, intelligente ex quo illa, et quam divino fonte manarent. Et Licentius: Sed dicendum, inquit, tibi est, ut beatus sit quisque, quid velle debeat, et quarum rerum eum oporteat habere desiderium. Invita me, inquam, natali tuo,

quando dignaberis; quidquid apposueris libenter sumam. Qua conditione hodie apud me ut epuleris peto, nec flagites quod fortasse non est paratum. Quem cum modestae ac verecundae commonitionis suae poeniteret: Ergo illud, inquam, convenit inter nos, neque quemquam beatum esse posse, qui quod vult non habet; neque omnem qui quod vult habet, beatum esse? Dederunt.

11. Quid illud, inquam, conceditis, omnem qui beatus non est, miserum esse? Non dubitaverunt. Omnis igitur, inquam, qui quod vult non habet, miser est. Placuit omnibus. Quid ergo sibi homo comparare debet, ut beatus sit, inquam? Forte enim etiam hoc isti nostro convivio subministrabitur, ne Licentii aviditas negligatur: nam id, opinor, ei comparandum est, quod cum vult, habet. Manifestum esse dixerunt. Id ergo, inquam, semper manens, nec ex fortuna pendulum, nec ullis subjectum casibus esse debet. Nam quidquid mortale et caducum est, non potest a nobis quando volumus, et quamdiu volumus haberi. Assentiebantur omnes. Sed Trygetius: Sunt, inquit, multi fortunati, qui eas ipsas res fragiles casibusque subjectas, tamen jucundas pro hac vita cumulate largeque possideant, nec quidquam illis eorum quae volunt desit. Cui ego: Qui timet, inquam, videturne tibi beatus esse? Non videtur, inquit. Ergo quod amat quisque si amittere potest, potestne non timere? Non potest, inquit. Amitti autem possunt illa fortuita. Non igitur haec qui amat et possidet, potest ullo modo beatus esse. Nihil repugnavit. Hoc loco autem mater: Etiamsi securus sit, inquit, ea se omnia non esse amissurum, tamen talibus satiari non poterit. Ergo et eo miser, quo semper est indigus. Cui ego: Quid, inquam, his omnibus abundans rebus atque circumfluens, si cupiendi modum sibi statuat, eisque contentus decenter jucundeque perfruatur; nonne tibi videtur beatus? Non ergo, inquit, illis rebus, sed animi sui moderatione beatus est. Optime, inquam, nec huic interrogationi aliud, nec abs te aliud debuit responderi. Ergo nullo modo dubitamus, si quis beatus esse statuit, id eum sibi comparare debere quod semper manet, nec ulla saeviente fortuna eripi potest. Hoc, inquit, Trygetius, jamdudum consensimus. Deus, inquam, vobis aeternus, et semper manens videtur? Hoc quidem inquit Licentius, ita certum est, ut interroga-

tione non egeat; caeterique omnes pia devotione concinuerunt. Deum igitur, inquam, qui habet, beatus est.

12. Quod cum gaudentes libentissime acciperent: Nihil ergo, inquam, nobis jam quaerendum esse arbitror, nisi quis hominum habeat Deum; beatus enim profecto is erit. De quo quaero quid vobis videatur. Hic Licentius: Deum habet, qui bene vivit. Trygetius: Deum habet, inquit, qui facit quae Deus vult fieri. In cujus sententiam Lastidianus concessit. Puer autem ille minimus omnium: Is habet Deum, ait, qui spiritum immundum non habet. Mater vero omnia, sed hoc maxime approbavit. Navigius tacebat. Quem cum interrogassem quid sentiret, illud ultimum sibi placere respondit. Nec Rusticum percontari visum est negligendum, quaenam esset de re tanta ejus sententia, qui mihi videbatur non deliberatione magis quam pudore impeditus silere; Trygetio consensit.

13. Tum ego: Teneo, inquam, omnium placita de re magna sane, et ultra quam nec quaeri quidquam oportet, nec inveniri potest, si modo eam, uti coepimus, serenissime ac sincerissime investigemus. Quod hodie quia longum est, et habent in epulis suis et animi quamdam luxuriem, si ultra modum in eas et voraciter irruant (ita enim male quodammodo digerunt; unde valetudini mentium non minus quam ab illa ipsa fame metuendum est), melius nos haec quaestio cras esurientes, si videtur, accipiet. Illud modo libenter liguriatis volo, quod subito mihi ministratori vestro in mentem suggestum est inferendum; et est, nisi fallor, qualia solent ultima apponi, quasi scholastico melle confectum atque conditum. Quo audito sese omnes quasi in elatum ferculum tetenderunt, coegeruntque ut dicere properarem quidnam id esset. Quid, inquam, putatis, nisi cum Academicis totum quod susceperamus confectum esse negotium? Quo accepto nomine, tres illi quibus res nota erat, sese erexerunt alacrius; et velut porrectis, ut fit, manibus inferentem ministrum adjuverunt, quibus potuerunt verbis, nihil se jucundius audituros esse monstrantes.

14. Tum ego ita rem proposui. Si manifestum est, inquam, beatum non esse qui quod vult non habet, quod paulo ante ratio demonstravit; nemo autem quaerit quod invenire non vult, et quaerunt illi semper

veritatem: volunt ergo invenire; volunt igitur habere inventionem veritatis. At non inveniunt: sequitur eos non habere quod volunt; et ex eo sequitur etiam beatos non esse. At nemo sapiens, nisi beatus: sapiens igitur Academicus non est. Hic repente illi, quasi totum rapientes exclamaverunt. Sed Licentius attentius et cautius advertens timuit assensionem, atque subjecit: Rapui quidem vobiscum, siquidem exclamavi illa conclusione commotus. Sed nihil hinc admittam in viscera, et partem meam servabo Alypio: nam aut simul eam mecum lambet, aut me admonebit cur non oporteat attingere. Dulcia, inquam, magis metuere Navigius deberet, splene vitioso. Hic ille arridens: Plane, inquit, me talia sanabunt. Nam nescio quomodo contortum hoc et aculeatum, quod posuisti, ut ait ille, de melle Hymetio, acriter dulce est, nihilque inflat viscera. Quare totum etiam, palato aliquantum remorso, tamen ut possum libentissime in medullas trajicio. Non enim video quomodo redargui possit ista conclusio. Prorsus nullo modo potest, inquit Trygetius. Quare gaudeo jamdiu cum illis me inimicitias suscepisse. Nam nescio qua impellente natura, vel, ut verius dicam, Deo, etiam nesciens quomodo refellendi essent, tamen eis nimis adversabar.

15. Hic Licentius: Ego, inquit, illos nondum desero. Ergo, ait Trygetius, dissentis a nobis? Numquidnam, ille inquit, vos ab Alypio dissentitis? Cui ego: Non dubito, inquam, quin si adesset Alypius, huic ratiunculae cederet. Non enim tam absurde sentire poterat, ut aut beatus ille videretur, qui tantum bonum animi, quod ardentissime vellet habere, non haberet, aut illos nolle invenire veritatem, aut eum qui beatus non sit esse sapientem: nam his tribus, quasi melle, farre, atque nucleis, illud quod metuis gustare, confectum est. Illene, inquit, huic tam parvae puerorum illecebrae cederet, Academicorum tanta ubertate deserta, qua inundante hoc nescio quid breve aut obruetur, aut pertrahetur? Quasi vero, inquam, longum aliquid nos quaeramus, praesertim adversus Alypium: nam non mediocriter parva ista esse fortia et utilia, satis sibi ipse de suo corpore argumentaretur. Tu autem qui elegisti de absentis auctoritate pendere, quid horum non probas? Utrum beatum non esse, qui quod vult non habet? an illos negas velle

habere inventam veritatem, quam vehementer inquirunt? an videtur tibi quisquam sapiens non beatus? Prorsus beatus est, inquit, qui quod vult non habet, quasi stomachanter arridens. Quod cum juberem ut scriberetur: Non dixi, inquit exclamans. Quod item cum annuerem scribi: Dixi, inquit. Atque ego semel praeceperam ut nullum verbum praeter litteras funderetur. Ita adolescentem inter verecundiam atque constantiam exagitatum tenebam.

16. Sed cum his verbis eum jocantes, quasi ad vescendam particulam suam provocaremus, animadverti caeteros rei totius ignaros, sed scire cupientes quid inter nos solos tam jucunde ageretur, sine risu nos intueri. Qui mihi prorsus similes visi sunt, quod plerumque fieri solet, iis qui cum epulantur inter avidissimos rapacissimosque convivas, a rapiendo vel gravitate sese abstinent, vel pudore terrentur. Et quia ego invitaveram, et magni cujusdam hominis personam, atque ut totum explicem, veri hominis etiam in illis epulis invitatorem gerebam, sustinere non potui, commovitque me illa inaequalitas mensae nostrae et discrepantia. Arrisi matri. Atque illa liberrime quod minus habebant, quasi de suo cellario promendum imperans: Jam dic nobis, inquit, et redde qui sint isti Academici, et quid sibi velint? Cui breviter cum exposuissem aperteque, ita ut nemo illorum ignarus abscederet: Isti homines, inquit, caducarii sunt (quo nomine vulgo apud nos vocantur, quos comitialis morbus subvertit), et simul surrexit ut abiret; atque hic omnes laeti ac ridentes, interposito fine discessimus.

CAPUT III.-- *Disputatio secundae diei. Quis Deum habeat eo modo ut beatus sit. Spiritus immundus duobus modis appellari solet.*

17. Postridie autem cum item post prandium, sed aliquanto quam pridie serius, iidem ibidemque consedissemus: Tarde, inquam, venistis ad convivium: quod vobis non cruditate accidisse arbitror, sed paucitatis ferculorum securitate; quod non tam mature aggrediendum visum est, quod cito vos peresuros putastis. Non multum enim reliquiarum credendum erat remansisse, ubi die ipso atque solemnitate tam exiguum repertum erat. Fortasse recte. Sed quid vobis praeparatum sit, ego quoque vobiscum nescio. Alius est enim qui om-

nibus cum omnes, tum maxime tales epulas praebere non cessat: sed nos ab edendo, vel imbecillitate, vel saturitate, vel negotio plerumque cessamus: quem manentem in hominibus beatos eos facere, inter nos heri, ni fallor, pie constanterque convenerat. Nam cum ratio demonstrasset eum beatum esse qui Deum haberet, nec huic quisquam vestrum sententiae restitisset, quaesitum est quisnam vobis videretur Deum habere. De qua re, si bene memini, tres sententiae dictae sunt. Nam parti placuit, Deum habere illum qui ea faceret quae Deus vellet. Quidam autem dixerunt quod is Deum haberet, qui bene viveret. Reliquis vero in eis Deus esse visus est, in quibus qui immundus appellatur, spiritus non est.

18. Sed fortasse omnes diversis verbis unum idemque sensistis. Nam si duo prima consideremus, et omnis qui bene vivit, ea facit quae vult Deus; et omnis qui ea facit quae vult Deus, bene vivit; nec quidquam est aliud bene vivere, quam ea facere quae Deo placeant: nisi quid vobis aliud videtur. Assentiebantur. Tertium vero illud paulo diligentius considerandum est, propterea quod ritu castissimorum sacrorum spiritus immundus, quantum intelligo, duobus modis appellari solet: vel ille qui extrinsecus invadit animam sensusque conturbat, et quemdam hominibus infert furorem; cui excludendo qui praesunt, manum imponere vel exorcizare dicuntur, hoc est, per divina eum adjurando expellere: aliter autem dicitur spiritus immundus, omnis omnino anima immunda; quod nihil est aliud quam vitiis et erroribus inquinata. Itaque abs te quaero, tu puer, qui fortasse aliquanto seneriore ac purgatiore spiritu istam sententiam protulisti, quis tibi videatur immundum spiritum non habere: illene qui daemonem non habet, quo vesani homines fieri solent; an ille qui animam suam a vitiis omnibusque peccatis mundavit? Is mihi videtur, inquit, immundum spiritum non habere, qui caste vivit. Sed castum, inquam, quem vocas? eumne qui nihil peccat, an eum qui ab illicito tantum concubitu temperet? Quomodo, inquit, castus potest esse, qui ab illicito tantum concubitu abstinens sese, caeteris peccatis non desinit inquinari? Ille est vere castus, qui Deum attendit, et ad ipsum solum se tenet. Quae rerba pueri sicut dicta erant, cum conscribi mihi placuisset: Is ergo, inquam,

necesse est ut bene vivat, et qui bene vivit necessario talis est; nisi quid tibi aliud videtur. Concessit cum caeteris. Ergo una est hic, inquam, dicta sententia.

19. Sed illud a vobis paululum quaero, velitne Deus ut homo Deum quaerat? Dederunt. Item quaero; numquidnam possumus dicere, illum qui Deum quaerit, male vivere? Nullo modo, dixerunt. Etiam hoc tertium respondete; spiritus immundus potestne Deum quaerere? Negabant, aliquantum dubitante Navigio, qui postea caeterorum vocibus cessit. Si igitur, inquam, qui Deum quaerit, id facit quod Deus vult, et bene vivit, et spiritum immundum non habet; qui autem Deum quaerit, nondum habet Deum: non igitur quisquis aut bene vivit, aut quod vult Deus facit, aut spiritum immundum non habet, continuo Deum habere credendus est. Hic cum se caeteri concessionibus suis deceptos riderent, postulavit mater, cum diu stupida fuisset, ut ei hoc ipsum quod conclusionis necessitate intorte dixeram, explicando relaxarem atque solverem. Quod cum factum esset: Sed nemo, inquit, potest pervenire ad Deum, nisi Deum quaesierit. Optime, inquam. Tamen qui adhuc quaerit, nondum ad Deum pervenit, etiamsi bene vivit. Non igitur quisquis bene vivit, Deum habet. Mihi, inquit, videtur Deum nemo non habere: sed eum qui bene vivit, habet propitium; qui male, infestum. Male igitur, inquam, hesterno die concessimus eum beatum esse qui Deum habet: siquidem omnis homo Deum habet, nec tamen omnis homo beatus est. Adde ergo, inquit, propitium.

20. Saltem, inquam, hoc inter nos satis constat, eum beatum esse qui habet propitium Deum? Vellem, inquit Navigius, consentire: sed illum vereor qui adhuc quaerit; praesertim ne concludas beatum esse Academicum, qui hesterno sermone, vulgari quidem et male latino, sed aptissimo sane, ut mihi videtur, verbo caducarius nominatus est. Non enim possum dicere homini Deum quaerenti adversum Deum esse: quod si dici nefas est, propitius erit; et qui propitium Deum habet, beatus est. Beatus ergo erit ille qui quaerit: omnis autem quaerens nondum habet quod vult. Erit igitur beatus homo qui quod vult non habet, quod heri nobis omnibus videbatur absurdum; unde credebamus Academicorum tenebras esse discussas. Quare jam de nobis

Licentius triumphabit; mihique illa dulcia, quae contra valetudinem meam temere accepi, has de me poenas exigere, quasi prudens medicus admonebit.

21. Hic cum etiam mater arrisisset: Ego, inquit, frygetius, non concedo continuo Deum adversari cui non sit propitius, sed esse aliquid medium puto. Cui ego: Istum tamen hominem, inquam, medium, cui nec Deus propitius est nec infestus, Deum quoquo modo habere concedis? Hic cum ille cunctaretur: Aliud est, inquit mater, Deum habere, aliud non esse sine Deo. Quid ergo, inquam, melius est; utrum habere Deum, an non esse sine Deo? Quantum, inquit, possum intelligere, ista est sententia mea: qui bene vivit, habet Deum, sed propitium; qui male, habet Deum, sed adversum. Qui autem adhuc quaerit, nondumque invenit, neque propitium neque adversum, sed non est sine Deo. Haeccine, inquam, vestra etiam sententia est? Hanc esse dixerunt. Dicite mihi, quaeso, inquam: non vobis videtur esse homini Deus propitius cui favet? Esse confessi sunt. Non ergo, inquam, favet Deus quaerenti sese homini? Responderunt: Favet. Habet igitur, inquam, qui Deum quaerit, Deum propitium; et omnis qui habet Deum propitium, beatus est. Beatus est ergo et ille qui quaerit. Qui autem quaerit, nondum habet quod vult. Erit igitur beatus qui quod vult non habet. Prorsus, inquit mater, non mihi videtur beatus esse qui quod vult non habet. Ergo, inquam, non omnis qui habet Deum propitium, beatus est. Si hoc cogit ratio, inquit, non possum negare. Ista igitur, inquam, distributio erit, ut omnis qui jam Deum invenit et propitium Deum habeat, et beatus sit: omnis autem qui Deum quaerit propitium Deum habeat, sed nondum sit beatus; jamvero quisquis vitiis atque peccatis a Deo se alienat, non modo beatus non sit, sed ne Deo quidem vivat propitio.

22. Quod cum placuisset omnibus: Bene habet, inquam; sed adhuc illud vereor, ne vos moveat quod jam superius concesseramus, miserum esse quisquis beatus non sit: cui consequens erit esse miserum hominem qui propitium tenet Deum, quem adhuc Deum quaerentem nondum diximus esse beatum. An vero, quod ait Tullius, multorum in terris praediorum dominos divites appellamus; omnium

virtutum possessores pauperes nominabimus? Sed illud videte, utrum quomodo verum est quod omnis egens miser sit, ita sit verum quod omnis miser egeat. Ita enim erit verum, nihil aliud esse miseriam quam egestatem, quod me nunc, cum diceretur, laudare sensistis. Hoc autem hodie longum est ut quaeramus; quare peto ne fastidio vobis sit ad istam mensam cras etiam convenire. Quod cum omnes se libentissime habere dixissent, surreximus.

CAPUT IV.-- *Disputatio tertiae diei. De quaestione pridie proposita dicendum. Miser est omnis qui eget. Sapiens porro aliquo non eget. An omnis qui miser est, egeat. Animi egestas. Animi plenitudo. Quis demum sit beatus.*

23. Tertius autem dies disputationis nostrae, matutinas nubes quae nos cogebant in balneas, dissipavit, tempusque pomeridianum candidissimum reddidit. Placuit ergo in pratuli propinqua descendere, atque omnibus nobis ubi commodum visum est considentibus, reliquus ita sermo peractus est. Omnia pene, inquam, quae interroganti mihi concedi a vobis volui, habeo ac teneo: quare hodierno die, quo possimus tandem hoc nostrum convivium aliquo intervallo dierum distinguere, aut nihil, aut non multum erit, ut opinor, quod mihi vos respondere necesse sit. Dictum enim erat a matre, nihil aliud esse miseriam quam egestatem, convenitque inter nos, omnes qui egeant miseros esse. Sed utrum omnes etiam miseri egeant, nonnulla quaestio est, quam hesterno die non potuimus explicare. Hoc autem ita se habere, si ratio demonstraverit, perfectissime inventum est qui sit beatus: erit enim ille qui non eget. Omnis enim non miser, beatus est. Beatus est ergo qui egestate caret, si quam dicimus egestatem, eamdem miseriam esse constiterit.

24. Quid enim, ait Trygetius? non potest ex eo jam confici, omnem non egentem beatum esse, quo manifestum est omnem qui egeat esse miserum? Nam concessisse nos memini, nihil esse medium inter miserum et beatum. Aliquidne, inquam, inter mortuum et vivum tibi medium videtur esse? nonne omnis homo aut vivus aut mortuus est? Fateor, inquit, neque hic esse aliquid medium: sed quorsum istud? Quia, inquam, etiam istud te fateri credo, omnem qui ante annum

sepultus est, esse mortuum. Non negabat. Quid? omnis qui ante annum sepultus non est, vivit? Non, ait, sequitur. Ergo, inquam, non sequitur ut si omnis qui eget miser est, omnis qui non eget sit beatus, quamvis inter miserum et beatum, ut inter vivum et mortuum, medium nihil inveniri queat.

25. Quod cum aliqui eorum paulo tardius intellexissent, me id quibus potui verbis ad eorum sensum accommodatis aperiente atque versante: Ergo, inquam, miserum esse omnem qui egeat, dubitat nemo: nec nos terrent quaedam sapientium corpori necessaria. Non enim eis eget ipse animus, in quo posita est vita beata. Ipse enim perfectus est; nullus autem perfectus aliquo eget: et quod videtur corpori necessarium sumet, si adfuerit; si non adfuerit, non eum istarum rerum franget inopia. Omnis namque sapiens fortis est; nullus autem fortis aliquid metuit. Non igitur metuit sapiens aut mortem corporis, aut dolores, quibus pellendis vel vitandis vel differendis sunt necessaria illa, quorum ei potest contingere inopia. Sed tamen non desinit eis bene uti, si ipsa non desunt. Verissima est enim illa sententia: Nam tu quod vitare possis stultum admittere est. (Terent. in Eunucho, act. 4, scen. 6) Vitabit ergo mortem ac dolorem, quantum potest et quantum decet; ne si minime vitaverit, non ex eo miser sit quia haec accidunt, sed quia vitare cum posset, noluit: quod manifestum stultitiae signum est. Erit ergo ista non vitans, non earum rerum perpessione, sed stultitia miser. Si autem non valuerit evitare, cum id sedulo ac decenter egerit, non eum ista irruentia miserum facient. Etenim et illa ejusdem comici sententia non minus vera est: Quoniam non potest id fieri quod vis, Id velis quod possit. (Id. in Andria, act. 2, scen. 1.) Quomodo erit miser, cui nihil accidit praeter voluntatem? Quia quod sibi videt non posse provenire, non potest velle. Habet enim rerum certissimarum voluntatem, id est, ut quidquid agit, non agat nisi ex virtutis quodam praescripto et divina lege sapientiae, quae nullo ab eo pacto eripi possunt.

26. Jam nunc videte, utrum etiam omnis qui miser est, egeat. Nam huic sententiae concedendae difficultatem illa res facit, quod multi in magna fortuitarum rerum copia constituti sunt, quibus ita facilia sunt omnia, ut ad eorum nutum praesto sit quidquid cupiditas poscit.

Difficilis quidem ista vita est. Sed fingamus aliquem talem, qualem Tullius fuisse dicit Oratam. Quis enim facile dicat Oratam egestate laborasse, hominem ditissimum, amoenissimum, deliciosissimum, cui neque ad voluptatem quidquam defuit, neque ad gratiam, neque ad bonam integramque valetudinem? Nam et praediis quaestuosissimis et amicis jucundissimis, quantum libuit, abundavit; et illis omnibus aptissime ad salutem corporis usus est, ejusque (ut breviter totum explicem) omne institutum voluntatemque omnem successio prospera consecuta est. Sed fortasse inquiet aliquis vestrum, plus illum quam habebat, habere voluisse. Hoc ignoramus. Sed quod satis est quaestioni, faciamus eum non desiderasse amplius quam tenebat. Videturne vobis eguisse? Etiamsi concedam, inquit Licentius, nihil eum desiderasse, quod in homine non sapiente nescio quomodo accipiam; metuebat tamen, erat enim vir, ut dicitur, ingenii non mali, ne illa omnia sibi vel uno adverso impetu raperentur. Non enim magnum erat intelligere, talia cuncta, quantacumque essent, esse sub casibus constituta. Tum ego arridens: Vides, inquam, Licenti, fortunatissimum istum hominem a beata vita ingenii bonitate impeditum. Quo enim erat acutior, eo videbat illa omnia se posse amittere; quo metu frangebatur, illudque vulgare satis asserebat: Infidum hominem malo suo esse cordatum.

27. Hic cum et ille et caeteri arrisissent: Illud tamen, inquam, diligentius attendamus, quia etsi timuit iste, non eguit: unde quaestio est. Egere est enim in non habendo, non in timore amittendi quae habeas. Erat autem iste miser, quia metuebat, quamvis non egeret. Non igitur omnis qui miser est, eget. Quod cum approbavisset cum caeteris etiam ipsa cujus sententiam defendebam, aliquantulum tamen addubitans: Nescio, inquit, tamen, et nondum plene intelligo quomodo ab egestate possit miseria, aut egestas a miseria separari. Nam et iste qui dives et locuples erat, et nihil, ut dicitis, amplius desiderabat; tamen quia metuebat, ne amitteret egebat sapientia. Ergone hunc egentem diceremus, si egeret argento et pecunia; cum egeret sapientia, non diceremus? Ubi cum omnes mirando exclamassent, me ipso etiam non mediocriter alacri atque laeto, quod ab ea potissimum dictum esset

quod pro magno de philosophorum libris, atque ultimum proferre paraveram: Videtisne, inquam, aliud esse multas variasque doctrinas, aliud animum attentissimum in Deum? Nam unde ista quae miramur, nisi inde procedunt? Hic Licentius laetus exclamans: Prorsus, inquit, nihil verius, nihil divinius dici potuit. Nam et major et miserabilior egestas nulla est, quam egere sapientia; et qui sapientia non eget, nulla re omnino egere potest.

28. Est ergo animi egestas, inquam, nihil aliud quam stultitia. Haec est enim contraria sapientiae, et ita contraria ut mors vitae, ut beata vita miserae; hoc est, sine aliquo medio. Nam ut omnis non beatus homo miser est, omnisque homo non mortuus vivit; sic omnem non stultum manifestum est esse sapientem. Ex quo et illud jam licet videre, non ex eo tantum Sergium Oratam fuisse miserum, quod timebat ne fortunae illa munera amitteret, sed quia stultus erat. Quo fit ut miserior esset, si tam pendulis nutantibusque iis quae bona putabat, nihil omnino metuisset. Esset enim non fortitudinis excubiis, sed mentis sopore securior, et altiore stultitia demersus miser. At si omnis qui caret sapientia magnam patitur egestatem, omnisque compos sapientiae nihilo eget, sequitur ut stultitia sit egestas. Ut autem omnis stultus miser, ita omnis miser stultus est. Ergo ut omnis egestas miseria, ita omnis miseria egestas esse convincitur.

29. Quam conclusionem Trygetius cum se parum intellexisse diceret: Quid, inquam, inter nos ratione convenit? Eum egere, inquit, qui sapientiam non habeat. Quid est ergo, inquam, egere? Sapientiam, inquit, non habere. Quid est, inquam, sapientiam non habere? Hic cum taceret, nonne hoc est, inquam, habere stultitiam? Hoc, inquit. Nihil est ergo aliud, inquam, habere egestatem, quam stultitiam; ex quo jam necesse est egestatem alio verbo nominari, quando stultitia nominatur. Quanquam nescio quomodo dicamus, Habet egestatem, aut, habet stultitiam. Tale est enim ac si locum aliquem, qui lumine careat, dicamus habere tenebras: quod nihil est aliud quam lumen non habere. Non enim tenebrae quasi veniunt aut recedunt; sed carere lumine hoc ipsum est jam tenebrosum esse, ut carere veste hoc est esse nudum. Non enim veste accedente veluti aliqua res mobilis nu-

ditas fugit. Sic ergo dicimus aliquem habere egestatem, quasi dicamus habere nuditatem. Egestas enim verbum est non habendi. Quamobrem, ut quod volo explicem sicut possum, ita dicitur, Habet egestatem; quasi dicatur, Habet non habere. Itaque, si stultitiam ipsam veram et certam egestatem esse monstratum est, vide jam quaestionem quam susceperamus, utrum soluta sit. Dubitabatur enim inter nos, utrum cum appellaremus miseriam, nihil aliud quam egestatem nominaremus. Dedimus autem rationem, recte stultitiam vocari egestatem. Sicut ergo et omnis stultus miser, et omnis miser stultus est; ita necesse est non solum omnem qui egeat miserum, sed etiam omnem qui miser sit egentem esse fateamur. At si ex eo quod et omnis stultus miser est, et omnis miser stultus est, conficitur stultitiam esse miseriam; cur non ex eo quod et quisquis eget miser, et quisquis miser est egeat, nihil aliud miseriam quam egestatem esse conficimus?

30. Quod cum omnes ita esse faterentur: Illud jam, inquam, sequitur, ut videamus quis non egeat; is enim erit sapiens et beatus. Egestas autem stultitia est, egestatisque nomen: hoc autem verbum sterilitatem quamdam et inopiam solet significare. Attendite, quaeso, altius, quanta cura priscorum hominum, sive omnia, sive quod manifestum est, quaedam verba creata sunt, earum rerum maxime quarum erat notitia pernecessaria. Jam enim conceditis omnem stultum egere, et omnem qui egeat stultum esse: credo vos etiam concedere animum stultum esse vitiosum, omniaque animi vitia uno stultitiae nomine includi. Primo autem die hujus disputationis nostrae nequitiam dixeramus esse ab eo dictam quod nec quidquam sit, cui contrariam frugalitatem a fruge fuisse nominatam. Ergo in iis duobus contrariis, hoc est frugalitate atque nequitia, illa duo videntur eminere, esse et non esse. Egestati autem de qua quaestio est, quid putamus esse contrarium? Hic cum aliquantum cunctarentur: Si dicam, inquit Trygetius, divitias; video his paupertatem esse contrariam. Est quidem, inquam, vicinum. Nam paupertas et egestas unum atque idem accipi solent. Tamen aliud verbum inveniendum est, ne meliori parti desit unum vocabulum, ut cum illa pars paupertatis et egestatis nomine abundet, ex hac parte solum opponatur divitiarum nomen. Nihil enim absurdius

quam ut hic sit egestas vocabuli, ubi est contraria pars egestati. Plenitudo, inquit Licentius, si dici potest, videtur mihi recte opponi egestati.

31. Postea, inquam, de verbo quaeremus fortasse diligentius. Non enim hoc curandum est in inquisitione veritatis. Quamvis enim Sallustius lectissimus pensator verborum, egestati opposuerit opulentiam (Sallustius, de Bello Catilin.); tamen accipio istam plenitudinem. Non enim hic grammaticorum formidine laborabimus, aut metuendum est ne ab eis castigemur, quod incuriose utimur verbis, qui res suas nobis ad utendum dederunt. Ubi cum arrisissent: Ergo, quia mentes vestras, inquam, cum intenti estis in Deum, velut quaedam oracula non contemnere statui, videamus quid sibi velit hoc nomen; nam nullum accommodatius esse arbitror veritati. Plenitudo igitur et egestas contraria sunt: at etiam hic similiter, ut in nequitia et frugalitate, apparent illa duo, esse et non esse. Et si egestas est ipsa stultitia, plenitudo erit sapientia. Merito etiam virtutum omnium matrem multi frugalitatem esse dixerunt. Quibus consentiens Tullius etiam in populari oratione ait: Ut volet quisque accipiat: ego tamen frugalitatem, id est modestiam et temperantiam, virtutem esse maximam judico (Orat. pro Dejotaro). Prorsus doctissime ac decentissime: consideravit enim frugem, id est illud quod esse dicimus, cui est non esse contrarium. Sed propter vulgarem loquendi consuetudinem, qua frugalitas quasi parcimonia dici solet, duobus consequentibus quid senserit, illustravit, subjiciendo modestiam et temperantiam: et haec duo verba diligentius attendamus.

32. Modestia utique dicta est a modo, et a temperie temperantia. Ubi autem modus est atque temperies, nec plus est quidquam nec minus. Ipsa est igitur plenitudo, quam egestati contrariam posueramus, multo melius quam si abundantiam poneremus. In abundantia enim intelligitur affluentia et quasi rei nimium exuberantis effusio. Quod cum evenit ultra quam satis est, etiam ibi desideratur modus, et res quae nimia est, modo eget. Ergo nec ab ipsa redundantia egestas aliena est; a modo autem et plus et minus aliena sunt. Ipsam etiam opulentiam si discutias, invenies eam nihil aliud tenere quam modum. Nam

non nisi ab ope dicta est opulentia. Quomodo autem opitulatur, quod nimium est, cum incommodius sit saepe quam parum? Quidquid igitur vel parum vel nimium est, quia modo eget, obnoxium est egestati. Modus ergo animi sapientia est. Etenim sapientia contraria stultitiae non negatur, et stultitia egestas, egestati autem contraria plenitudo. Sapientia igitur plenitudo. In plenitudine autem modus. Modus igitur animi in sapientia est. Unde illud praeclarum est, et non immerito diffamatur hoc primum in vita esse utile: Ut ne quid nimis. (Terent. in Andria, act. 1, scen. 1.)

33. Dixeramus autem in exordio hodiernae disputationis nostrae, quod si inveniremus nihil aliud esse miseriam quam egestatem, eum beatum esse fateremur, qui non egeret. Est autem inventum: ergo beatum esse nihil est aliud quam non egere, hoc est esse sapientem. Si autem quaeritis quid sit sapientia (nam et ipsam ratio, quantum in praesentia potuit, evolvit atque eruit); nihil est aliud quam modus animi, hoc est, quo sese animus librat, ut neque excurrat in nimium, neque infra quam plenum est coarctetur. Excurrit autem in luxurias, dominationes, superbias, caeteraque id genus, quibus immoderatorum miserorumque animi sibi laetitias atque potentias comparari putant. Coarctatur autem sordibus, timoribus, moerore, cupiditate, atque aliis, quaecumque sunt, quibus homines miseros etiam miseri confitentur. Cum vero sapientiam contemplatur inventam, cumque, ut hujus pueri verbo utar, ad ipsam se tenet, nec se ad simulacrorum fallaciam, quorum pondus amplexus a Deo suo cadere atque demergi solet, ulla commotus inanitate convertit; nihil immoderationis, et ideo nihil egestatis, nihil igitur miseriae pertimescit. Habet ergo modum suum, id est sapientiam, quisquis beatus est.

34. Quae est autem dicenda sapientia, nisi quae Dei Sapientia est? Accepimus autem etiam auctoritate divina, Dei Filium nihil esse aliud quam Dei Sapientiam (I Cor. I, 24): et est Dei Filius profecto Deus. Deum habet igitur quisquis beatus est: quod omnibus nobis jam ante placuit, cum hoc convivium ingressi sumus. Sed quid putatis esse sapientiam, nisi veritatem? Etiam hoc enim dictum est: Ego sum Veritas (Joan. XIV, 6). Veritas autem ut sit, fit per aliquem summum modum,

a quo procedit, et in quem se perfecta convertit. Ipsi autem summo modo nullus alius modus imponitur: si enim summus modus per summum modum modus est, per seipsum modus est. Sed etiam summus modus necesse est ut verus modus sit. Ut igitur veritas modo gignitur, ita modus veritate cognoscitur. Neque igitur veritas sine modo, neque modus sine veritate unquam fuit. Quis est Dei Filius? Dictum est, Veritas. Quis est qui non habet patrem, quis alius quam summus modus? Quisquis igitur ad summum modum per veritatem venerit, beatus est. Hoc est animo Deum habere, id est Deo frui. Caetera enim quamvis a Deo habeantur, non habent Deum.

35. Admonitio autem quaedam, quae nobiscum agit, ut Deum recordemur, ut eum quaeramus, ut eum pulso omni fastidio sitiamus, de ipso ad nos fonte veritatis emanat. Hoc interioribus luminibus nostris jubar sol ille secretus infundit. Hujus est verum omne quod loquimur, etiam quando adhuc vel minus sanis vel repente apertis oculis audacter converti, et totum intueri trepidamus: nihilque aliud etiam hoc apparet esse quam Deum, nulla degeneratione impediente perfectum. Nam ibi totum atque omne perfectum est, simulque est omnipotentissimus Deus. Sed tamen quamdiu quaerimus, nondum ipso fonte, atque ut illo verbo utar, plenitudine saturati, nondum ad nostrum modum nos pervenisse fateamur: et ideo, quamvis jam Deo adjuvante, nondum tamen sapientes ac beati sumus. Illa est igitur plena satietas animorum, haec est beata vita, pie perfecteque cognoscere a quo inducaris in veritatem, qua veritate perfruaris, per quid connectaris summo modo. Quae tria unum Deum intelligentibus unamque substantiam, exclusis vanitatibus variae superstitionis, ostendunt. Hic mater recognitis verbis quae suae memoriae penitus inhaerebant, et quasi evigilans in fidem suam, versum illum sacerdotis nostri: Fove precantes, Trinitas, (Ambrosius in hym., Deus creator omnium.) laeta effudit, atque subjecit: Haec est nullo ambigente beata vita, quae vita perfecta est, ad quam nos festinantes posse perduci, solida fide, alacri spe, flagrante charitate praesumendum est.

36. Ergo, inquam, quoniam modus ipse nos admonet, convivium aliquo intervallo dierum distinguere, quantas pro viribus possum gra-

tias ago summo et vero Deo Patri, Domino liberatori animarum: deinde vobis qui concorditer invitati, multis etiam me cumulastis muneribus. Nam tantum in nostrum sermonem contulistis, ut me negare non possim, ab invitatis meis esse satiatum. Hic omnibus gaudentibus et laudantibus Deum: Quam vellem, inquit Trygetius, hoc modo nos quotidie pasceres. Modus, inquam, ille ubi

This work was produced in association with:

www.ingramcontent.com/pod-product-compliance
Lightning Source LLC
LaVergne TN
LVHW061049070526
838201LV00074B/5230